■SCHOLASTIC
News
Nonfiction Readers

Jane Goodall

by
Jo S. Kittinger

Children's Press®
A Division of Scholastic Inc.
New York Toronto London Auckland Sydney
Mexico City New Delhi Hong Kong
Danbury, Connecticut

These content vocabulary word builders
are for grades 1-2.

Consultant: Diane M. Doran
Associate Professor
Department of Anthropology
The State University of New York at Stony Brook

Curriculum Specialist: Linda Bullock

Photo Credits:

Photographs © 2005: Corbis Images: back cover (Karl Ammann), 5 bottom right, 14 (Anthony Bannister/Gallo Images), 7 (Ashley Cooper), 5 top left, 8, 20 bottom left, 21 center right (Martin Harvey/Gallo Images), 22, 23 top right (Karen Huntt), cover (Kennan Ward), 6 (Garth Webber); Getty Images/Michael K. Nichols/National Geographic: 4 bottom left, 12; National Geographic Image Collection: 1, 4 bottom right, 13, 17, 19 (Michael Nichols), 5 top right, 11, 20 right, 21 left (Baron Van Lawick); NHPA/Martin Harvey: 2, 20 left center; Photo Researchers, NY: 5 bottom left, 15 (Mary Beth Angelo), 21 bottom right (Tony Camacho), 23 top left, 23 bottom left (Tom McHugh), 21 top right (Phil McLean/Holt Studios International); The Image Works/Tom Brakefield: 23 bottom right.

Map by Matt Kania

Book Design: Simonsays Design!

Library of Congress Cataloging-in-Publication Data

Kittinger, Jo S.
    Jane Goodall / by Jo S. Kittinger.
        p. cm. — (Scholastic news nonfiction readers)
    Includes bibliographical references (p.   ) and index.
    ISBN 0-516-24940-1 (lib. bdg.)   0-516-24783-2 (pbk.)
    1. Goodall, Jane, 1934- —Juvenile literature. 2. Primatologists—
        England—Biography—Juvenile literature. 3. Chimpanzees—
        Research—Juvenile literature. I. Title. II. Series.
QL31.G58K58 2005
590'.92

2005002102

CONTENTS

WORD HUNT

Look for these words as you read. They will be in **bold**.

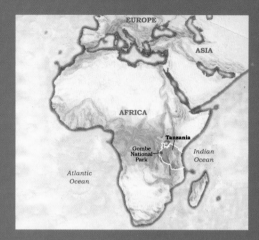

Africa
(**af**-ruh-kuh)

hoot
(hoot)

Jane Goodall
(jane goodawl)

chimpanzee
(chim-**pan**-zee)

David Greybeard
(**day**-vid **gray**-beerd)

mound
(mound)

termite
(**tur**-mite)

Have you ever seen a hen lay an egg?

Jane Goodall did!

When she was a child, she waited in a henhouse.

Then she saw it happen. A hen laid an egg!

Jane loved learning about animals.

Look! This hen has laid eggs in its nest.

When Jane grew up, she went to Tanzania, **Africa**.

She worked at a park.

She studied **chimpanzees** there.

It was not easy.

chimpanzee

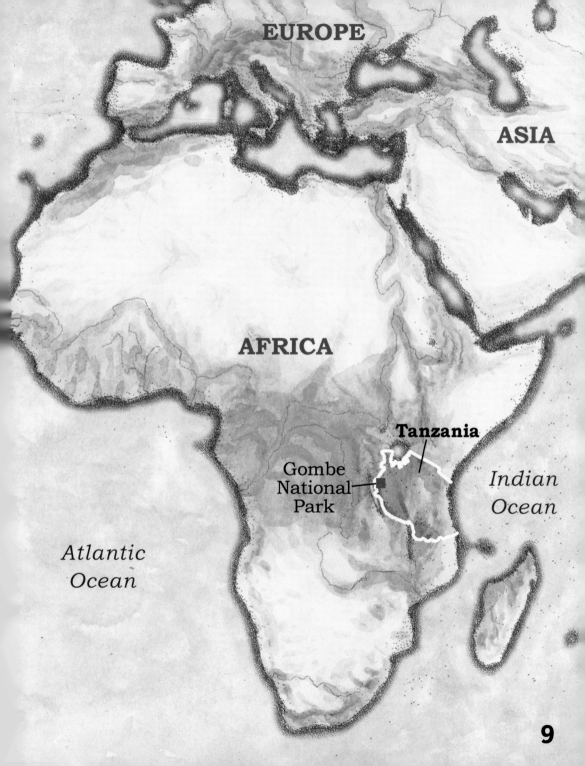

EUROPE

ASIA

AFRICA

Tanzania

Gombe
National
Park

*Indian
Ocean*

*Atlantic
Ocean*

9

At first, the chimpanzees ran away from Jane.

Then, one chimp let Jane get close.

Jane named him **David Greybeard**.

Soon, other chimpanzees let Jane get close, too.

David Greybeard likes
eating bananas.

Jane learned chimps show happiness, sadness, and fear.

Sometimes they hug and kiss.

When chimps talk to each other, they **hoot**, bark, and grunt.

chimp hooting

Jane watches Fifi pick bugs off of a baby chimp.

Jane studied chimps for many years.

She learned how chimps live and eat.

She saw chimps use sticks to get **termites** to eat.

Some termites live in **mounds**.

termites

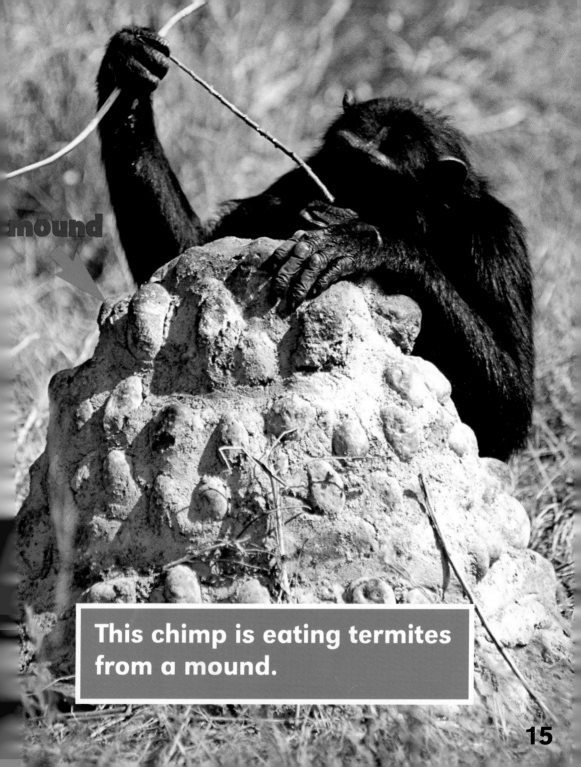

mound

This chimp is eating termites from a mound.

Jane saw that some baby chimps have no mother.

So, she opened an orphanage for these chimps.

An orphanage is a safe place for baby chimps to grow up.

This man works at the orphanage. He lets the baby chimps play outside.

Jane hates to see chimps in cages.

Samson has been in a cage for a long time. Jane visits him.

Jane works to keep all chimpanzees safe.

She hopes you will, too!

Jane visits Samson at a zoo in Kenya.

A CHIMP GROWS UP!

Like people, chimpanzees take many years to become adults.

1 This is a baby chimp. It stays close to its mother. The mother chimp feeds her baby.

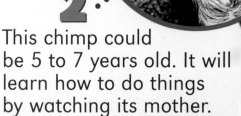

2 This chimp could be 5 to 7 years old. It will learn how to do things by watching its mother.

5 This chimp is old! Scientists still do not know how long chimps can live.

4 This chimp could be 13 to 33 years old. It is a grown-up with a baby of its own.

3 This chimp could be 8 to 13 years old. It spends time with adult chimps to learn new things.

21

YOUR NEW WORDS

Africa (**af**-ruh-kuh) a continent

chimpanzee (chim-**pan**-zee) a kind of
great ape

David Greybeard (day-vid **gray**-beerd)
the first chimpanzee that became
Jane's friend

hoot (hoot) one of the sounds chimps make to
talk to each other

Jane Goodall (jane goodawl) is a scientist
who studies chimpanzees

mound (mound) a hill or a pile

termite (**tur**-mite) an insect that eats wood

GREAT APES

There are four kinds of great apes.

bonobo

chimpanzee

gorilla

orangutan

INDEX

FIND OUT MORE
Book:
The Chimpanzees I Love, by Jane Goodall, Scholastic Press, 2001.

Website:
www.discoverchimpanzees.org

MEET THE AUTHOR:
Jo S. Kittinger writes books for children. Jo has had many pets. She also likes to watch birds. Raccoons, opossums, and squirrels visit her house. Jo lives in Hoover, Alabama.